PIANO | VOCAL | GUITAR · CD **VOLUME 27**

Piano Play-Along

HAL·LEONARD

ANDREW LLOYD WEBBER™ GREATS

CONTENTS

PAGE	TITLE	DEMO TRACK	PLAY-ALONG TRACK
2	Any Dream Will Do **Joseph and the Amazing Technicolor® Dreamcoat**	1	9
14	Don't Cry for Me Argentina **Evita**	2	10
22	I Don't Know How to Love Him **Jesus Christ Superstar**	3	11
26	The Music of the Night **The Phantom of the Opera**	4	12
32	The Phantom of the Opera **The Phantom of the Opera**	5	13
9	Unexpected Song **Song and Dance**	6	14
40	Whistle Down the Wind **Whistle Down the Wind**	7	15
44	With One Look **Sunset Boulevard**	8	16

Andrew Lloyd Webber™ is a trademark owned by Andrew Lloyd Webber.

ISBN 0-634-08965-X

HAL·LEONARD®
CORPORATION
7777 W. BLUEMOUND RD. P.O. BOX 13819 MILWAUKEE, WI 53213

Visit Hal Leonard Online at
www.halleonard.com

ANY DREAM WILL DO

from JOSEPH AND THE AMAZING TECHNICOLOR® DREAMCOAT

Music by ANDREW LLOYD WEBBER
Lyrics by TIM RICE

way   some - one was weep - ing,

but the world was sleep - ing,   an - y dream will

do.   I wore my coat

CHOIR:

I wore my

with gold - en lin - ing, bright col - ours

coat, _____ ah, _____

shin - ing won - der - ful and new.

ah, _____

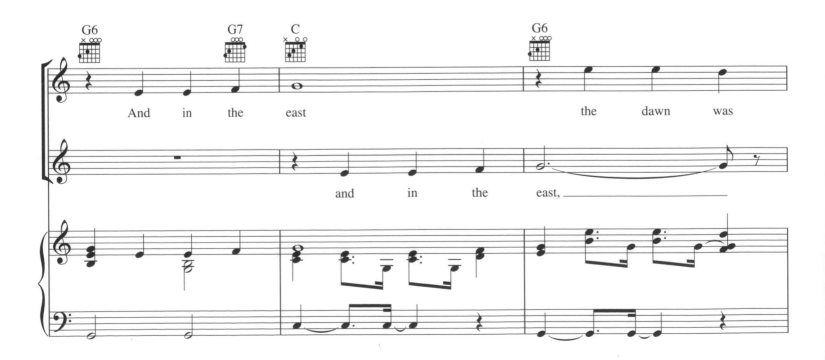

And in the east the dawn was

and in the east, _____

break - ing, and the world was wak - ing, ah, _____ ah, ___

an - y dream will do. _____

JOSEPH:

A

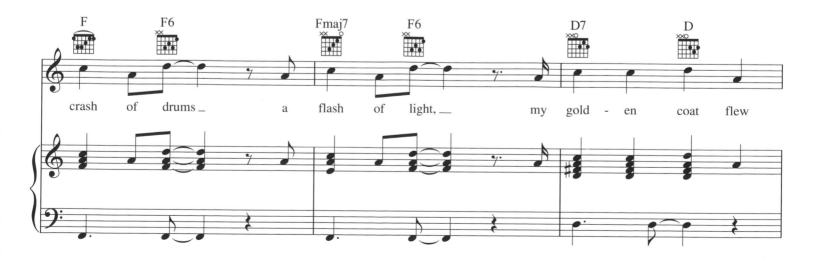

crash of drums _ a flash of light, _ my gold - en coat flew

out of sight. _ The col - ours fad - ed in - to dark - ness, I was left a -

CHOIR:

The col - ours fad - ed in - to dark - ness, ah, _____

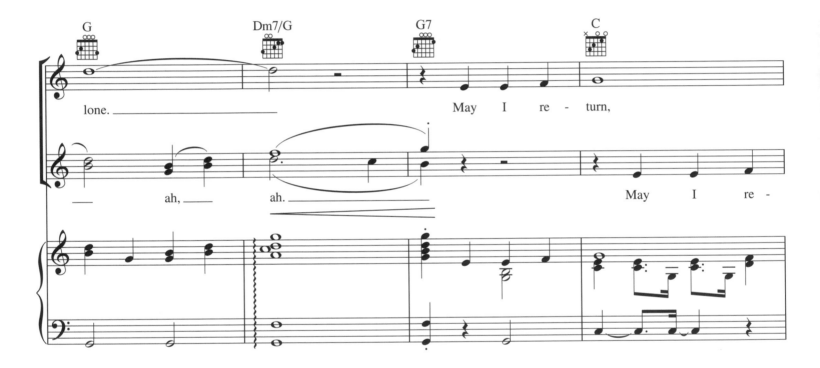

lone. _____ May I re - turn,

ah, _____ ah. _____ May I re -

to the be - gin - ning, the light is

turn, ah, _____

dim - ming and the dream is too,

ah. _____

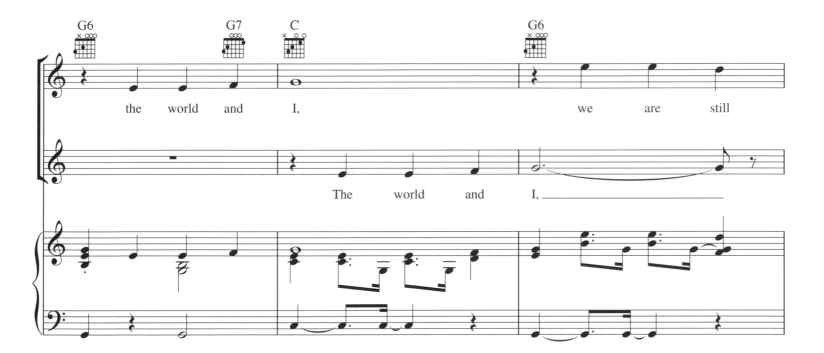

the world and I, we are still

The world and I, _____

wait - ing, still hes - i - tat - ing

ah, _____ ah. _____

UNEXPECTED SONG
from SONG AND DANCE

Music by ANDREW LLOYD WEBBER
Lyrics by DON BLACK

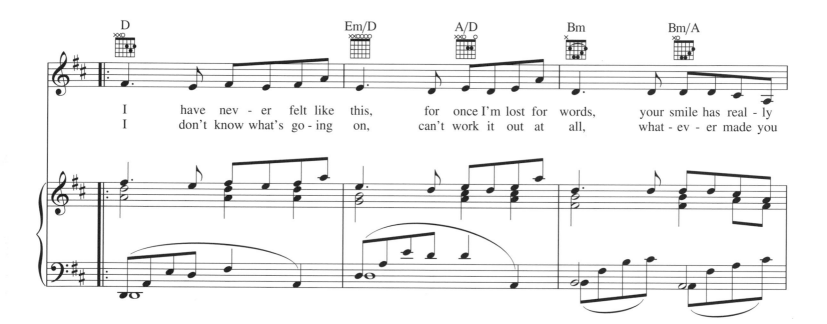

I have nev-er felt like this, for once I'm lost for words, your smile has real-ly
I don't know what's go-ing on, can't work it out at all, what-ev-er made you

thrown me. This is not like me at all, I nev-er thought I'd
choose me? I just can't be-lieve my eyes, you look at me as

know ____ the kind of love you've shown ____ me. }
though ____ you could-n't bear to lose ____ me. }

Now, ____ no mat-ter where I am, ____ no mat-ter what I do, ____ I see your face ap-

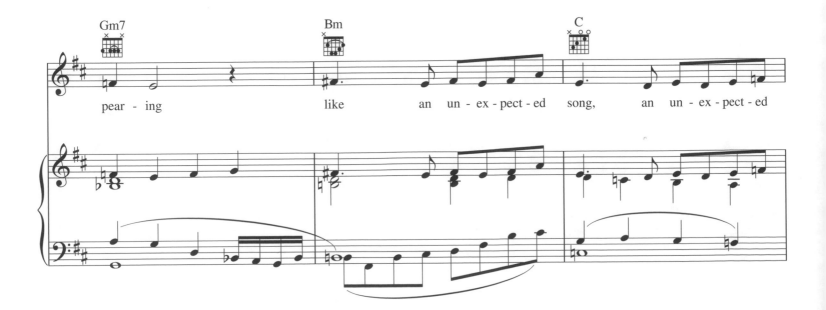

pear - ing ____ like ____ an un-ex-pect-ed song, ____ an un-ex-pect-ed

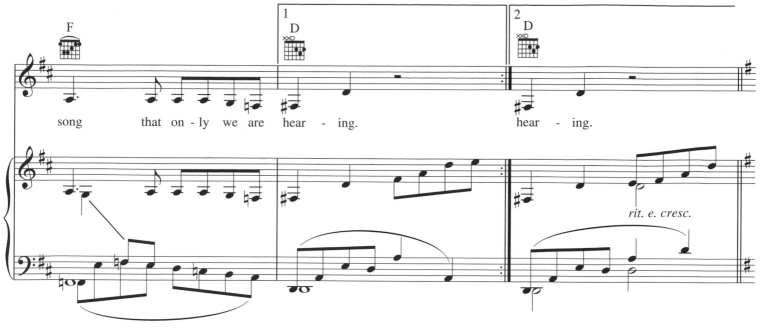

song that on - ly we are hear - ing. hear - ing.

I have nev - er felt like this, for once I'm lost for

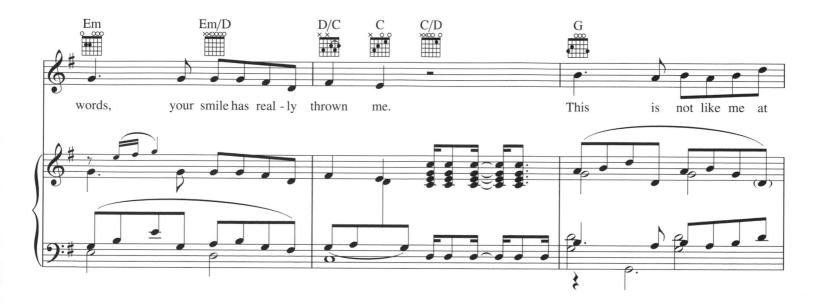

words, your smile has real - ly thrown me. This is not like me at

all, I nev-er thought I'd know the kind of love you've shown me.

Now, no mat-ter where I am, no mat-ter what I do, I see your face ap-

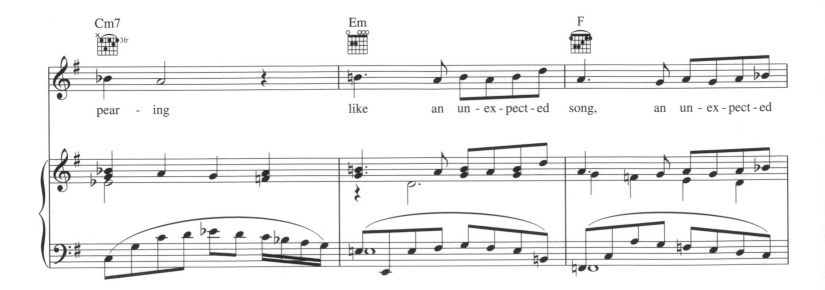

pear-ing like an un-ex-pect-ed song, an un-ex-pect-ed

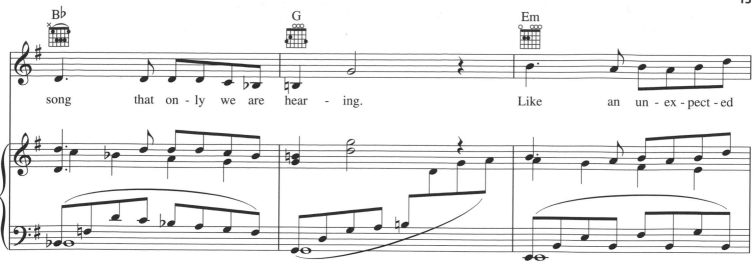

song that on-ly we are hear-ing. Like an un-ex-pect-ed

song, an un-ex-pect-ed song that on-ly we are hear-ing.

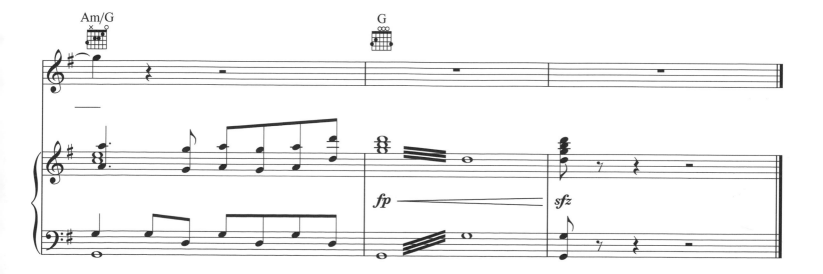

DON'T CRY FOR ME ARGENTINA

from EVITA

Words by TIM RICE
Music by ANDREW LLOYD WEBBER

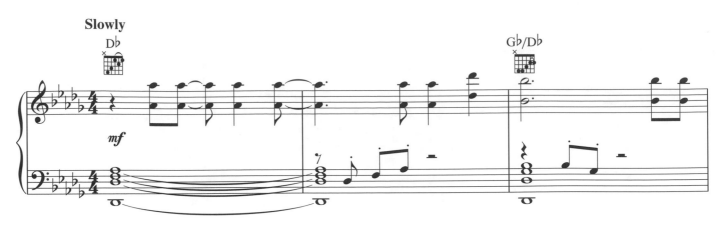

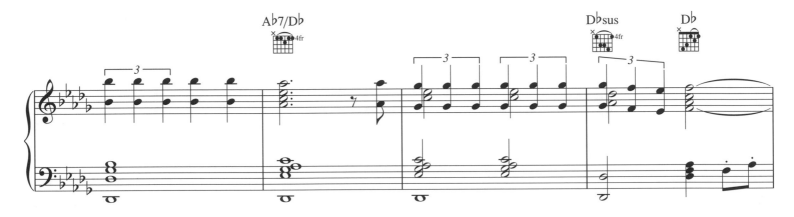

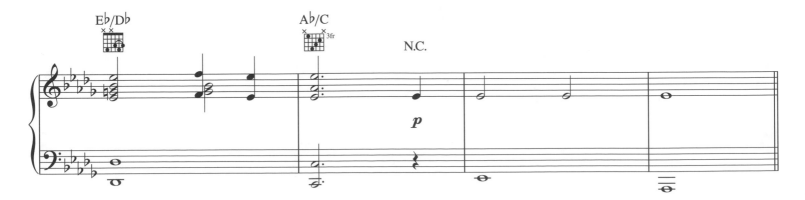

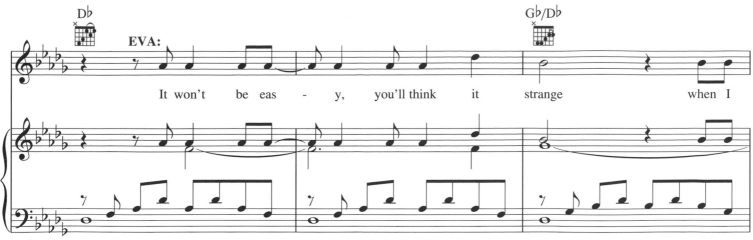

EVA:
It won't be eas - y, you'll think it strange when I

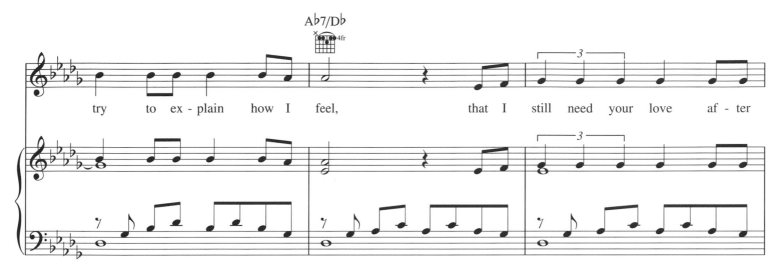

try to ex - plain how I feel, that I still need your love af - ter

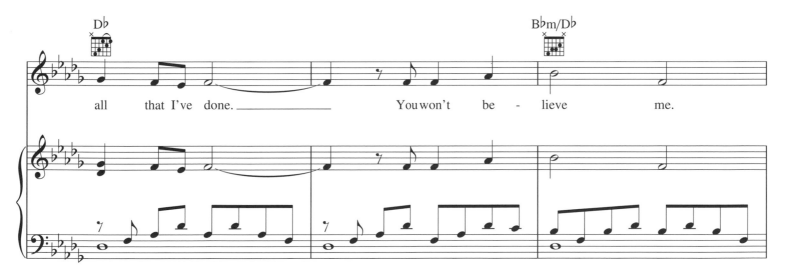

all that I've done. You won't be - lieve me.

All you will see is a girl you once knew, al - though she's dressed up to the

nines, at six-es and sev-ens with you.

poco rall.

I had to let it hap-pen, I had to change, could-n't spend all my life down at

p a tempo

heel, look-ing out of the win-dow, stay-ing out of the sun. So I chose

free-dom, run-ning a-round try-ing ev-'ry-thing new, but noth-ing im-pressed me at all,

I nev-er ex-pec-ted it to.

Don't cry for me Ar-gen-ti-na, _____ the truth is I nev-er

left you. __ All through my wild days, _____ my mad ex-is-tence, _____ I kept my

prom-ise, don't keep your dis-tance. _____

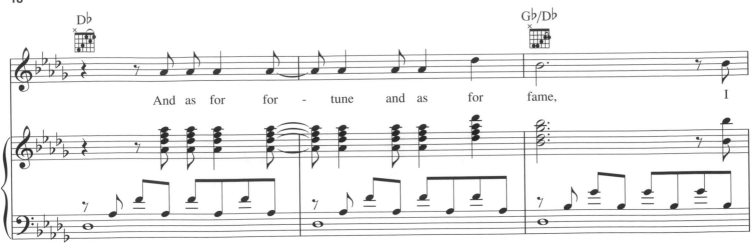

And as for for - tune and as for fame, I

nev - er in - vit - ed them in, though it seemed to the world _ they were

all I de - sired. They are il - lu - sions, they're

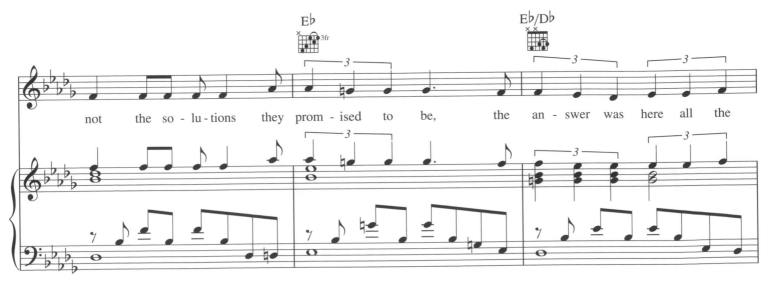

not the so - lu - tions they prom - ised to be, the an - swer was here all the

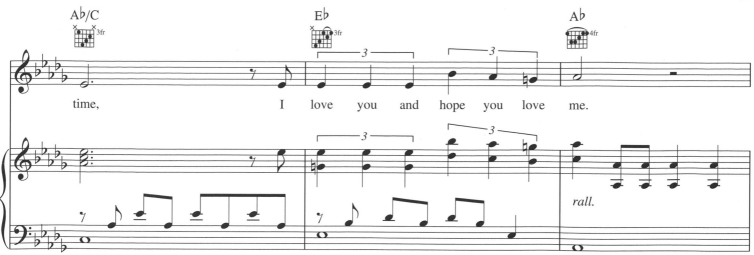

time, I love you and hope you love me.

Don't cry for me Ar-gen-ti-na. **CHOIR:** Mm _____

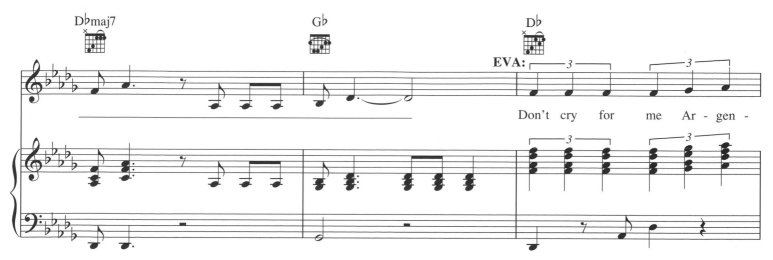

EVA: Don't cry for me Ar-gen-

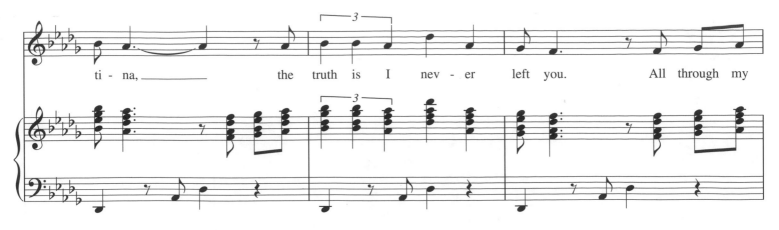

ti - na, _____ the truth is I nev - er left you. All through my

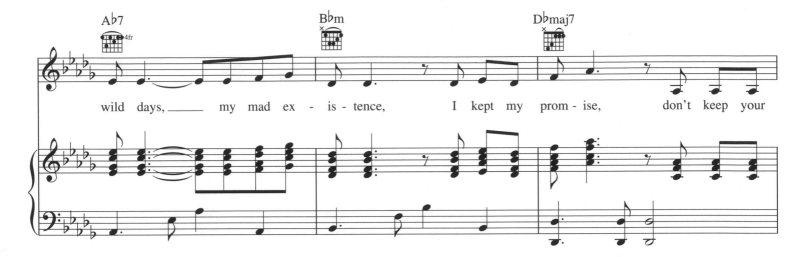

wild days, _____ my mad ex - is - tence, I kept my prom - ise, don't keep your

dis - tance. _____ Have I said too much, there's noth - ing more I can think of to

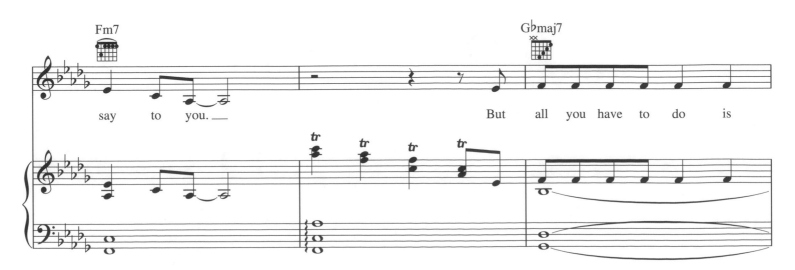

say to you. _____ But all you have to do is

look at me to know that ev -'ry word is true.__

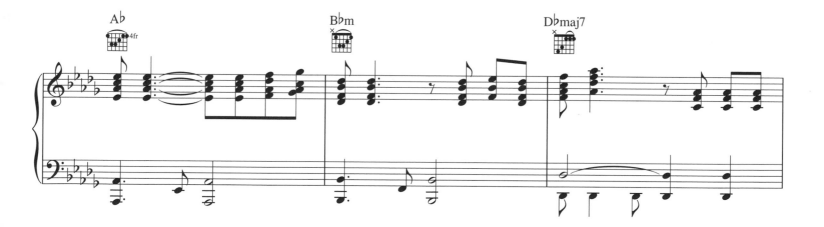

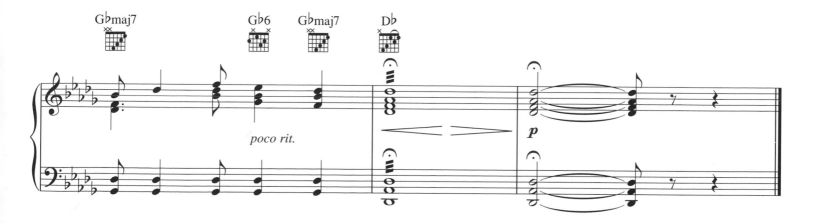

poco rit.

I DON'T KNOW HOW TO LOVE HIM

from JESUS CHRIST SUPERSTAR

Words by TIM RICE
Music by ANDREW LLOYD WEBBER

Slowly, tenderly and very expressively

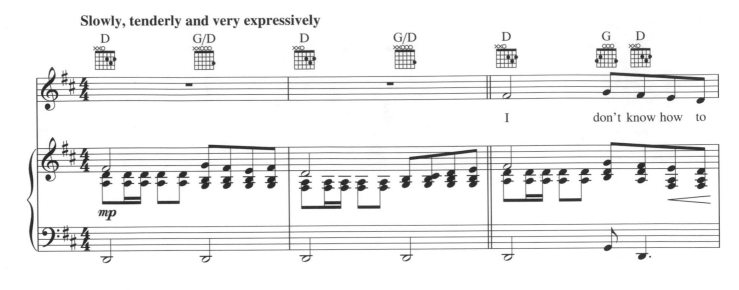

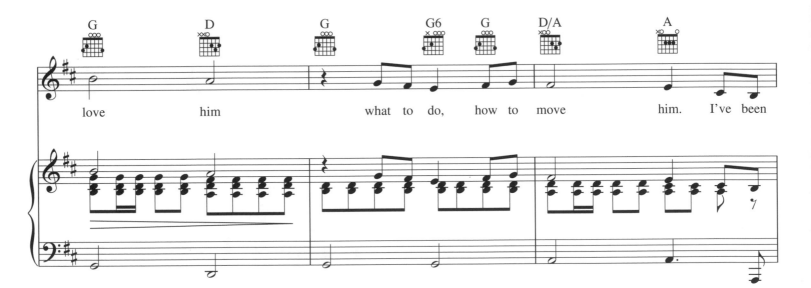

THE MUSIC OF THE NIGHT
from THE PHANTOM OF THE OPERA

Music by ANDREW LLOYD WEBBER
Lyrics by CHARLES HART
Additional Lyrics by RICHARD STILGOE

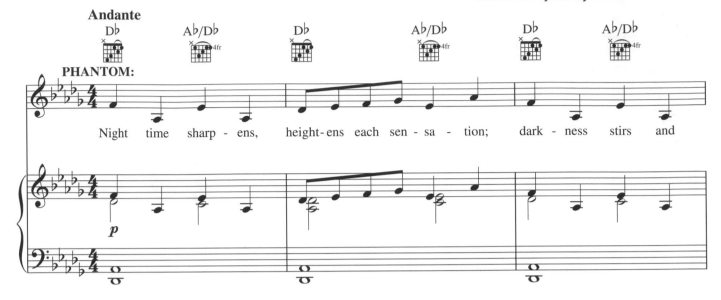

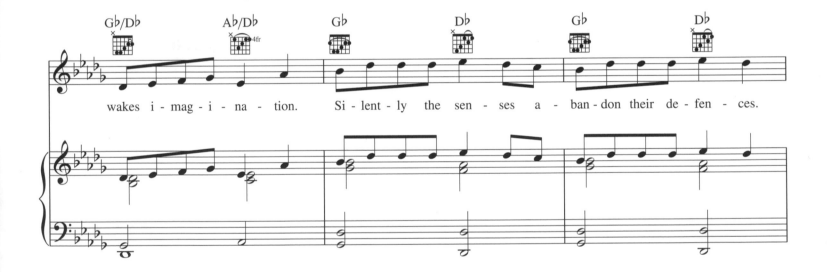

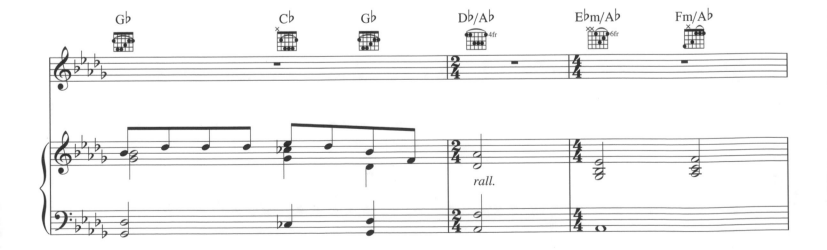

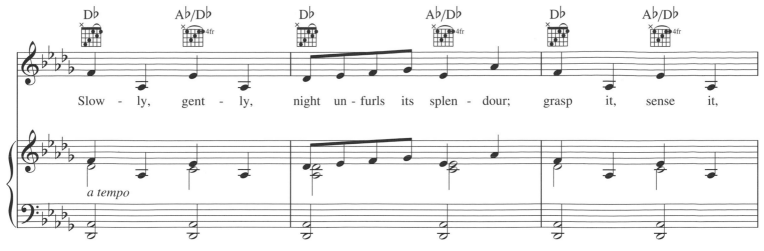

Slow - ly, gent - ly, night un - furls its splen - dour; grasp it, sense it,

a tempo

trem - u - lous and ten - der. Turn your face a - way from the gar - ish light of day, turn your

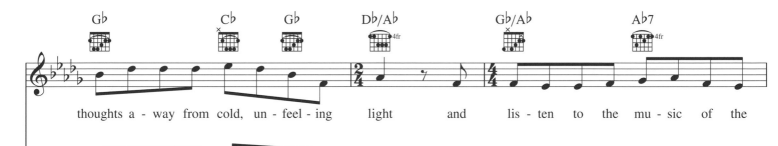

thoughts a - way from cold, un - feel - ing light and lis - ten to the mu - sic of the

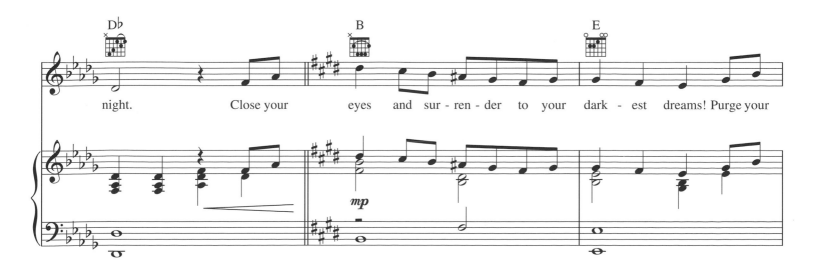

night. Close your eyes and sur - ren - der to your dark - est dreams! Purge your

mp

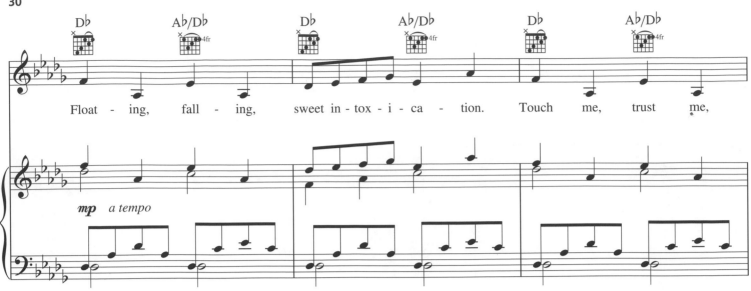

Float - ing, fall - ing, sweet in - tox - i - ca - tion. Touch me, trust me,

mp *a tempo*

sa - vour each sen - sa - tion. Let the dream be - gin, let your dark - er side give in to the

mf

pow - er of the mu - sic that I write, the pow - er of the mu - sic of the

rall.

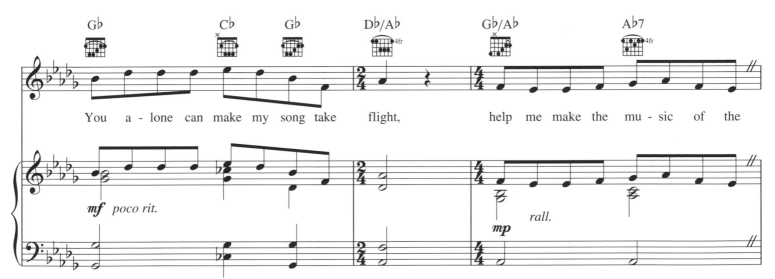

You a - lone can make my song take flight, help me make the mu - sic of the

Lento

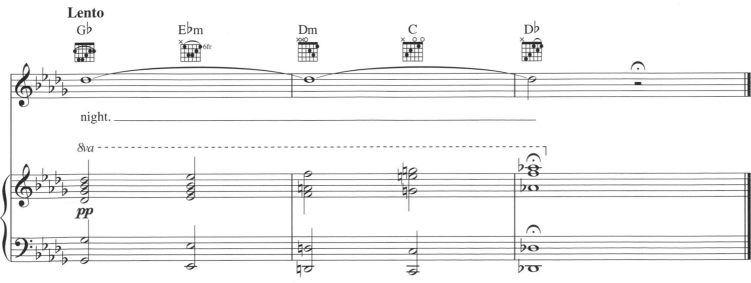

night.

THE PHANTOM OF THE OPERA

from THE PHANTOM OF THE OPERA

Music by ANDREW LLOYD WEBBER
Lyrics by CHARLES HART
Additional Lyrics by RICHARD STILGOE and MIKE BATT

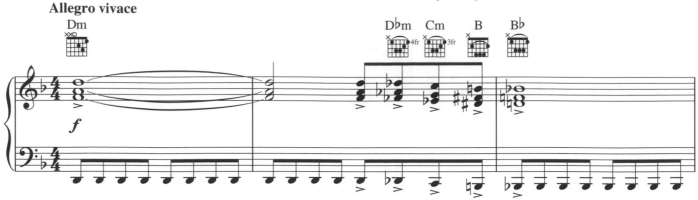

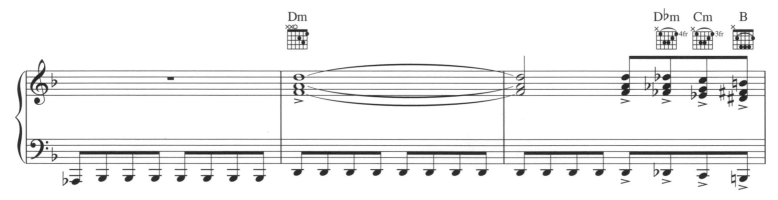

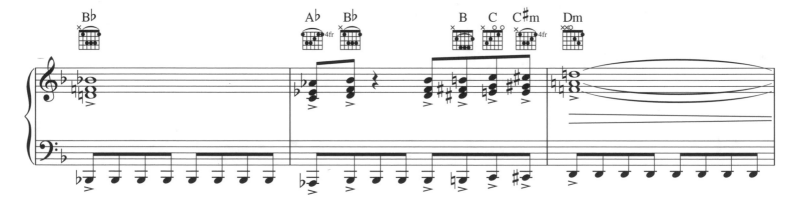

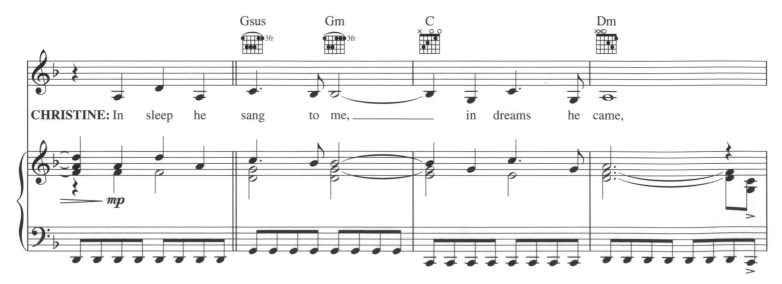

CHRISTINE: In sleep he sang to me, _____ in dreams he came,

that voice which calls to me _____ and speaks my name.

And do I dream a-gain? _____ for now I find _____

_____ the phan - tom of the op-er-a is

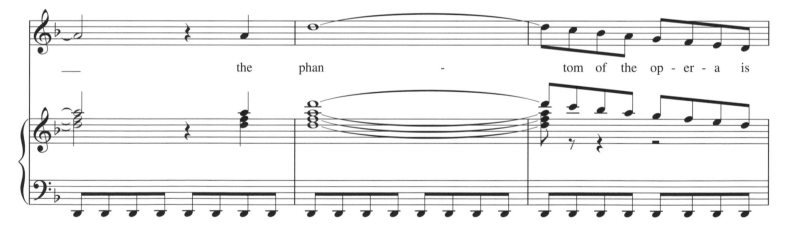

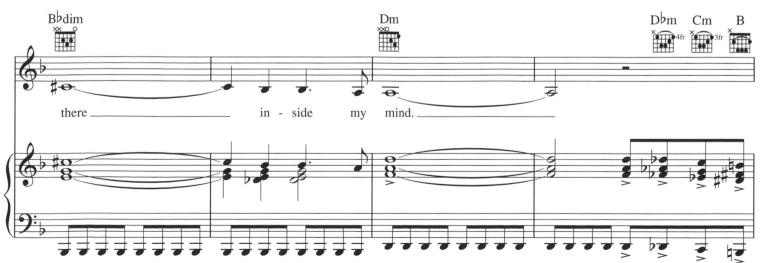

there _____ in - side my mind. _____

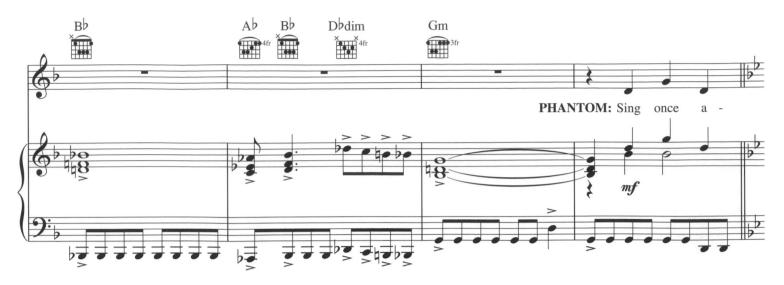

PHANTOM: Sing once a -

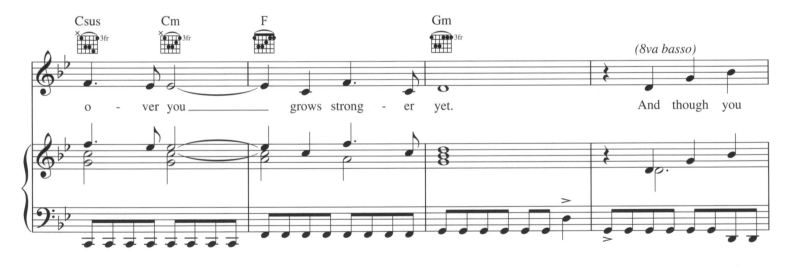

gain with me ____ our strange du - et; ____ my pow - er

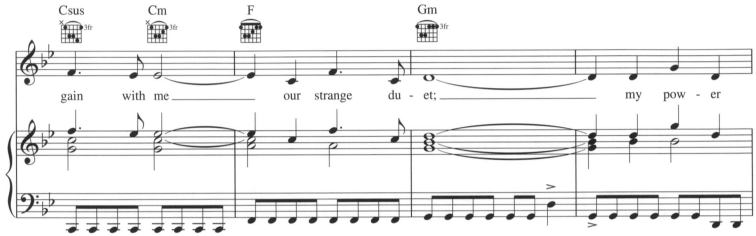

o - ver you ____ grows strong - er yet. And though you

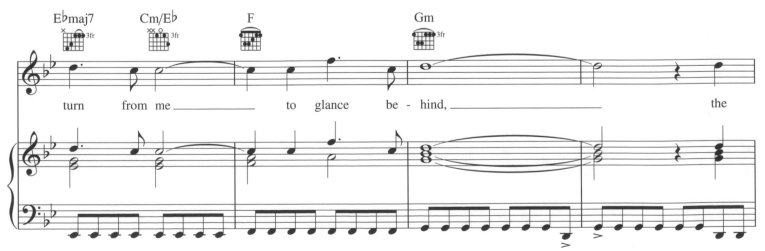

turn from me ____ to glance be - hind, ____ the

phan - tom of the op-er-a is there _____ in - side your

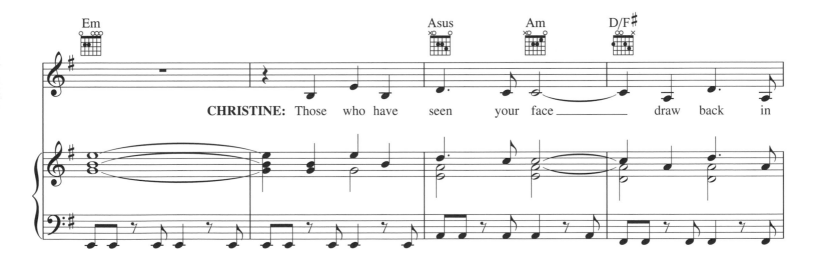

mind. _____

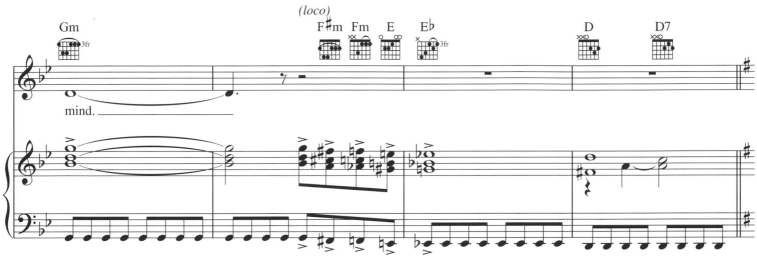

CHRISTINE: Those who have seen your face _____ draw back in

fear. _____ I am the mask you wear, _____ it's me they PHANTOM:

Em/B

hear. **PHANTOM & CHRISTINE:** Your spi - rit and my voice _____ in one com -
My spi - rit and your voice _____ in one com -

Cmaj7 **Am/C** **D**

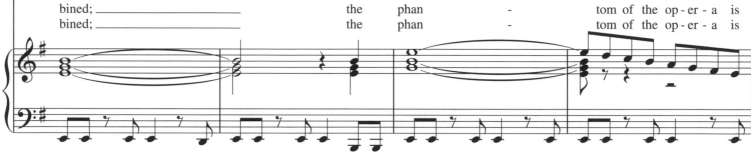

Em

bined; _____ the phan - tom of the op - er - a is
bined; _____ the phan - tom of the op - er - a is

Cdim **Em**

VOICES:

there in - side my mind. *He's there,* the phan - tom of the
there in - side your mind.

C **Em**

op - era. _____ *Be - ware* the phan - tom of the

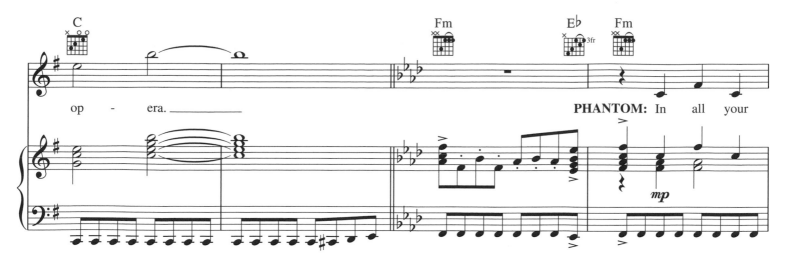

op - era. _____

PHANTOM: In all your

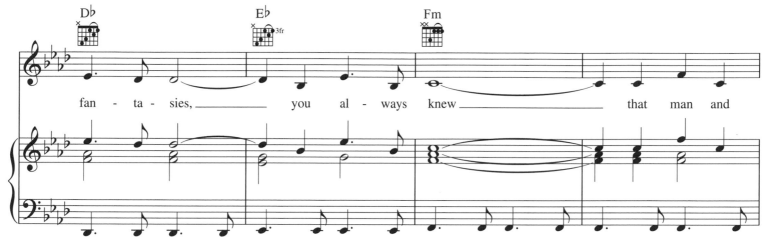

fan - ta - sies, _____ you al - ways knew _____ that man and

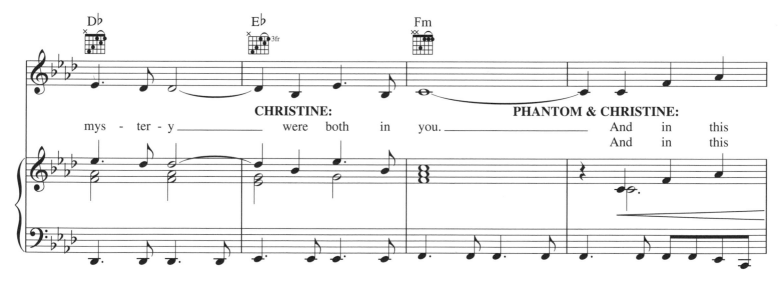

CHRISTINE:

mys - ter - y _____ were both in you. _____

PHANTOM & CHRISTINE:
And in this
And in this

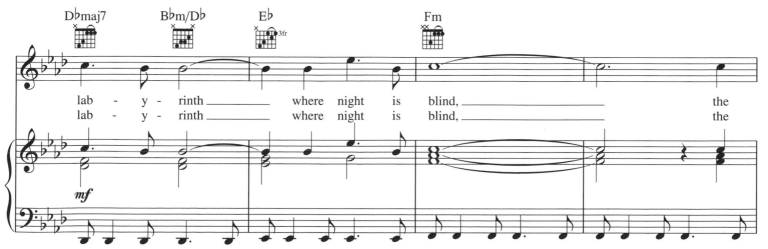

lab - y - rinth _____ where night is blind, _____ the
lab - y - rinth _____ where night is blind, _____ the

WHISTLE DOWN THE WIND

from WHISTLE DOWN THE WIND

Music by ANDREW LLOYD WEBBER
Lyrics by JIM STEINMAN

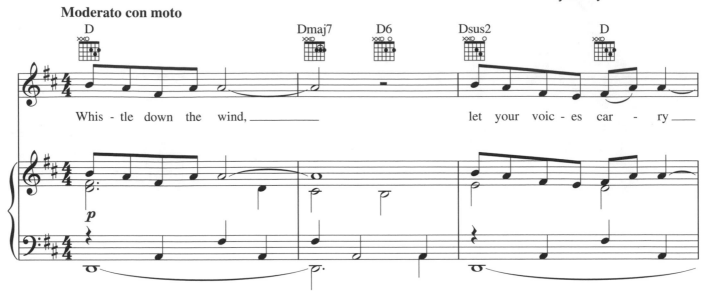

Moderato con moto

Whis-tle down the wind,_____ let your voic-es car-ry_____

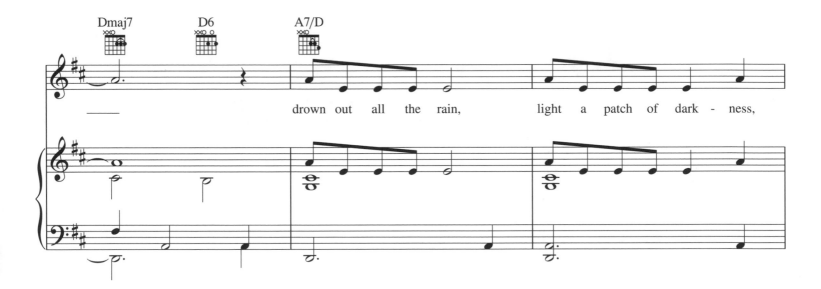

_____ drown out all the rain, light a patch of dark-ness,

treach-er-ous and scar-y._____ Howl_ at the stars,_____

whis - per when you're sleep - ing.

I'll be there to hold you, I'll be there to stop the chills and all the weep - ing.

Make it clear and strong so the whole night

long ev - 'ry sig - nal that you send, un - til the ver - y end

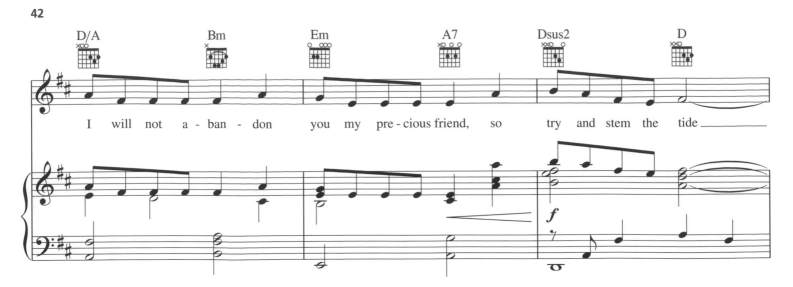

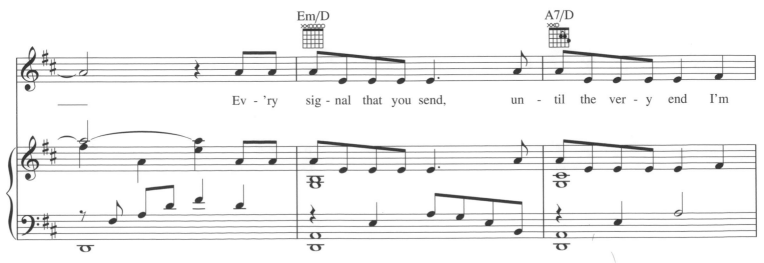

WITH ONE LOOK

from SUNSET BOULEVARD

Music by ANDREW LLOYD WEBBER
Lyrics by DON BLACK and CHRISTOPHER HAMPTON,
with contributions by AMY POWERS

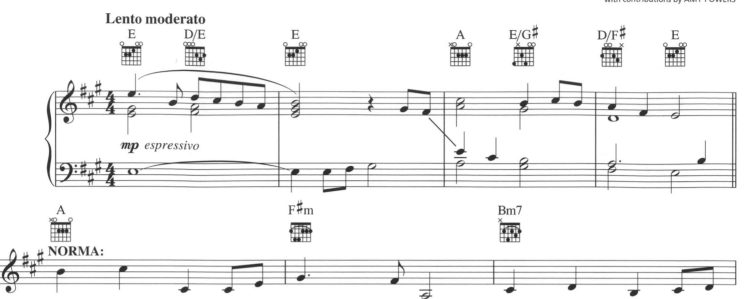

NORMA:

With one look I can break your heart, with one look I play

ev-ery part. I can make your sad heart sing, with one

look you'll know all you need to know. With one smile I'm the girl next door

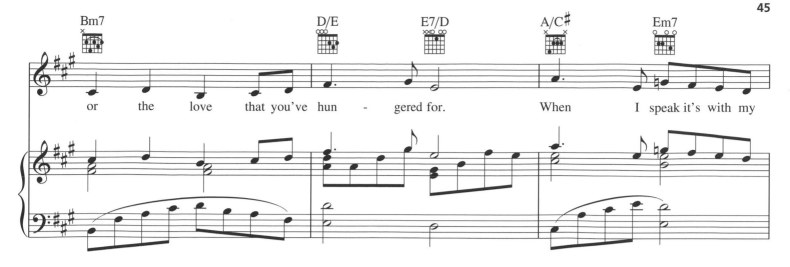

or the love that you've hun - gered for. When I speak it's with my

soul, I can play an - y role. No words can tell the

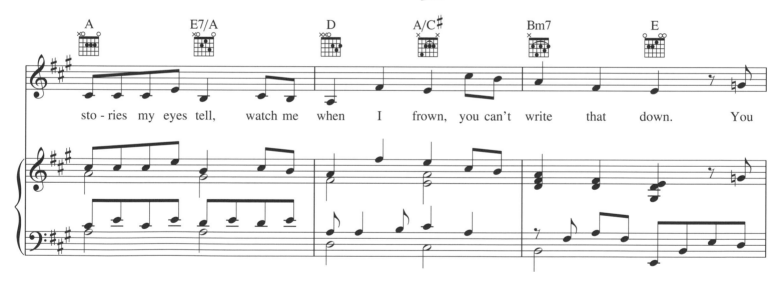

sto - ries my eyes tell, watch me when I frown, you can't write that down. You

know I'm right, it's there in black and white, when I look your way you'll hear

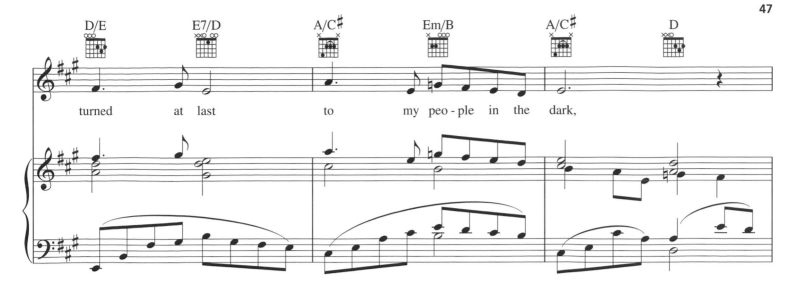

turned at last to my peo-ple in the dark,

still out there in the dark.

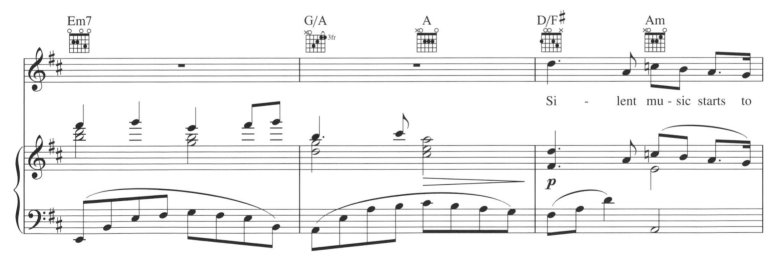

Si - lent mu - sic starts to

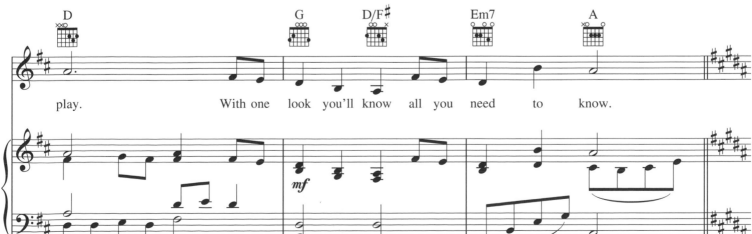

play. With one look you'll know all you need to know.

With one look I'll ig-nite a blaze, I'll re-turn to my

glo-ry days. They'll say Nor-ma's back at last.

This time I am stay-ing, I'm stay-ing for good, I'll be back where I was born to

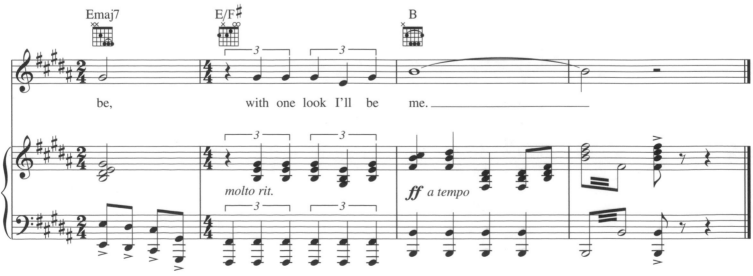

be, with one look I'll be me.